For Ben and John

Cover picture: The hot wind in the Sudan keeps Mabruka's kite in the air. She made it with her friends in Kindergarten.

Oxfam would like to acknowledge, with thanks, the following photographers:

Toby Adamson (cover and pages 18–19), Howard Davies (pages 24–25), Sarah Errington (pages 8–9), Julio Etchart (pages 6–7), Jim Holmes (20–21), Crispin Hughes (pages 22–23) Rhodri Jones (pages 10–11), Jenny Matthews (pages 5 and 16–17), Rajendra Shaw (12–13), Alex Smailes (14–15) and Gisèle Wulfsohn (26–27).

The book begins on page 6.

Playtime copyright © Frances Lincoln Limited 2006
Text copyright © Kate Petty 2006
Photographs copyright © Oxfam Activities Limited
and the photographers as named 2006

The right of Kate Petty to be identified as the Author of this work has been asserted by her in accordance with the Copyright, Designs and Patents Act, 1988.

First published in Great Britain in 2006 by
Frances Lincoln Children's Books, 4 Torriano Mews, Torriano Avenue, London NW5 2RZ

www.franceslincoln.com

British Library Cataloguing in Publication Data available on request

ISBN 10: 1-84507-332-0
ISBN 13: 978-1-84507-332-9

Printed in China

1 3 5 7 9 8 6 4 2

Oxfam GB will receive a 5% royalty for each copy of this book sold in the UK.

Playtime

Kate Petty

FRANCES LINCOLN CHILDREN'S BOOKS
in association with

 Oxfam

Cidinha and her friends have plenty of fun playing together outside their homes in Brazil. Which side do you think will win the tug-of-war?

I'm Cidinha — fourth from the left.

Winters are cold and snowy where Sasha lives in Russia. He has made a secret hidey-hole in the snow.

This snow house took a day to build.

Timo lives near the port of Timbuktu, in Mali. He and his friends have made toy boats. What do you think these boats are made from?

I hope it doesn't sink!

Shakeel's school is in Hyderabad, a hot and sandy part of India. He plays football in the shade with his friends.

Will I score a goal this time?

Giorgi and his friend live in Azerbaijan. They have fun racing the toy go-karts they made themselves.

You can steer the go-karts with the handles.

Gianni has made
himself a toy helicopter
from a plastic bottle.
He lives in Albania.

Look at my rotor
blades turning
in the wind!

The families of these boys
from the Sudan own lots
of animals – and the boys
like to model them in clay!

Can you see
a camel with
a basket?

Linh and his friend have made catapults from elastic bands. They are aiming at pebbles near Linh's home in Vietnam.

It hurts when the elastic snaps back at me!

The hot midday sun in Burkina Faso doesn't stop Alex and Astrid running races. Everyone cheers them on.

We are the best at running in our class!

After school, Paige can play on the swings in the park near her home in the United Kingdom. She learned to swing by herself when she was four.

I love flying through the air on a swing.

Nothando is playing a game like Jacks. She has to throw the biggest stone in the air and pick up as many little stones as she can before it comes down again.

Lots of children in South Africa play this game.

United Kingdom

Mali

Burkina Faso

Brazil

Russia

Albania

Azerbaijan

Sudan

India

Vietnam

South
Africa